24

34

40

46

# Foreword: Two Worlds Collide

Received wisdom has opposed fashion's fickle, fleeting and insubstantial character, with craft's perceived morality, timelessness and integrity. This position is now being challenged by the practice of fashion and craft as well as writing and thinking on these subjects.

Satellites of Fashion, a major survey of contemporary British hats, bags and shoes, is the first exhibition to celebrate the fusion between the two worlds of craft and fashion. It explains the design, making and meaning of avant-garde, crafted fashion accessories. It is about craft skills as the basis for innovation and creativity, and about obsession with detail. It embraces a diversity of materials.

Just as the world of fashion provides a liberating arena for the crafts, so craft skills provide an enormous and often unacknowledged creative resource for fashion. The exhibition asks questions about the role of craft in fashion, and the identity of the maker as craftsperson or fashion designer.

Claire Wilcox has brought to the subject an innovative, personal and serious intent. She has revealed how accessories are not led by fashion but are in its orbit, objects rich in texture and detail, which suggest a world of human emotions, hidden secrets and character acting. We are most grateful to her for her extensive research which has resulted in an exhibition which includes the work of established style leaders alongside small bespoke companies and introduces young, up-and-coming accessory makers, based from Belfast to Fife, from Glasgow to London. From all perspectives, their roots are in craft.

Satellites of Fashion is an opportunity to analyse individual objects, like rare species, up close and out of the retail context, and to observe more subtle issues to do with making. To emphasise the point that these objects have an alternative reading, the exhibition design by Urban Salon uses sound, light and movement. Hats flutter and spin, shoes talk and mumble, and bags contain sinister secrets. Mirrors positioned at head, torso and foot height allude to the body of the wearer (and visitor). Extended captions describe the exhibits through memories and views expressed by the exhibitors themselves, answering questions posed by the curator.

5

Our warmest gratitude is owed to all those who have been involved in this exhibition. We are most grateful to the exhibitors for not only making and lending new work but also for contributing their thoughts and insights. We are most fortunate to have drawn on the knowledge of two specialists in the field, Valerie Mendes, Chief Curator, Textiles and Dress Department, V&A, and co-selector of the exhibition, and Lou Taylor, Professor of Dress and Textile History, University of Brighton. Both acted as mentors to Claire during her research and we thank them for their advice and support. Thankyou finally to the design team, Urban Salon and Cartlidge Levene, to Richard Walmsley composer of the soundtrack, to photographer Gry Garness and exhibition organiser Beatrice Hosegood.

**Louise Taylor, Director of Exhibitions and Collection**

# Introduction

The aim of Satellites of Fashion is to explore the design, manufacture and meaning of British crafted fashion accessories. Rarely have accessories been exhibited in their own right, for they usually serve as afterthoughts to some larger exhibition, their voices silent. Liberated by their independence from clothes, hats, bags and shoes have a coherent language which is expressed in this exhibition through their craft identity. This identity is formed by an individualistic vision married to craft skills, a form of meiosis, or transformation, charged by fashion. Shoemaker Oliver Sweeney wrote, " 'Fashion' is part of the dream we sell; the dream doesn't work without quality and fit...'The Craft' ".

The potential for traditional skills to act as a vehicle for the conceptual and the modern is well understood in the world of couture for, in the bag maker Sonia Boriczewski's words, 'the skills of craft help push forward innovation in fashion'. Fashion designers often exploit the tension between traditionalism and modernity, and this is perhaps most obvious in the field of accessories in which traditional skills are so overt. These skills are celebrated and pushed to their limits by makers such as Bill Amberg who uses leather to form crisp dress folds, Victoria Brown who starts 'with a pile of fleece' from which she makes both felt and hat, and Manolo Blahnik whose stiletto heeled shoes find exquisite balance. As the hat maker Dai Rees explained 'we aim to prove that there is a place for the aesthetics and skills embodied in handmade pieces in this commercial and highly exposed field'.

Top fashion designers who work with shoemakers, handbag makers and milliners such as Adele Tipler, who described herself as 'a craftsperson whose milieu is the catwalk', use accessories to enhance their collections, recognising their ability to condense and intensify a look. As Nathalie Hambro stated, 'accessorising an outfit is the final punctuation of our sartorial message'. This rediscovery of the significance and power of accessories has had a direct impact upon their increasing availability. Not since the 1950s have they been deemed so vital, when it was observed that 'It is perhaps in fashion that the power of accessories is so absolute. They can heighten fashion, they can soften fashion. They can add fashion where before there was none. At times they *are* fashion'. ('Accent on Accessories', 1957)

The accessories in Satellites of Fashion operate at the extremities of dress, stylistically and physically. Worn at expressive points of the body, the head, feet and hands, accessories have the freedom to be fetishistic, theatrical, frivolous while also standing for craft, knowledge, creativity. Shoes provide the point of contact between body and ground, whether perilous or reassuring, and their construction mirrors the anatomical complexity of the foot. Always in pairs, complimenting and reflecting each other like twins, the shoe is doubly dangerous, for footwear fashion can also be podoerotic art. Enhancing the sensuality of the human gait, the shoe is experienced by the wearer through the 'fit' of its soft internal skin; as the psychologist Havelock Ellis wrote, 'Of all the forms of erotic symbolism, the most frequent is that which idealises the foot and shoe...'

Hats, the least functional and fittingly perhaps the most cerebral of accessories, sit at the furthest point from the shoe. Like a halo around the face, they focus attention on the eyes, the windows to the soul. The hat crowns the head, adding status, formality and height, sobriety or wit. Until very recently it was relegated to traditional social functions such as weddings, christenings and funerals. Jilli Blackwood's earliest memory is of a cold dining room in her grandmother's house, the table covered in decorative feathers, hats and hat blocks. Today, the hat has been reinvented; where once it was as essential as wearing gloves, it is now worn by choice for, as Fred Bare stated, 'Hats are wonderful dressing up clothes and, of course, they can disguise or flatter the wearer'.

The bag is the most personal and intimate accessory of all and for this reason, bags seem to evoke many memories. Sharon Porteus recalled her mother's handbag 'which had everything you could possibly need in it – rather like Mary Poppins' '. Without actually being fitted to the body, the bag is constantly in contact with the hands or torso, yet, left alone, it stands quite independently without losing its grace or meaning. While it is a functional object, it can also be expressive, aggressive, defensive. The bag is the vehicle for minute detail, fastidious zips and fastenings, secretive pockets, while its contents are a perennial mystery. Its exterior is a vehicle for embellishment, from Asta Barrington's embroidered handbags – inspired by wrought ironwork, old lace, biscuits, mosaics – to the soft, writhing surfaces of Hikaru Noguchi's woollen bags.

The hatter Victoria Brown wrote that 'Craft skills are vital to maintain the illusion of the object. The hat, shoe and bag must be so well made that the object (not the process) is the first thought, the synthesis of form, colour, surface. Craft skills can give a hat a timeless quality. Without craft skills fashion cannot develop or evolve, the craftsperson pushes materials and ideas in new directions and uses his or her skills and understanding of materials to discover new forms and methods of working'. To all the makers in Satellites of Fashion, traditional craft skills remain a central concern, even if, in Joanna Walker's words, they have a desire to 'pull everything down and create something new'. A sense of permanence and worth, against the transience of fashion, is expressed by the shoemaker Henrietta Park who wrote, 'I see myself as a designer craft person. My designs are not throwaway fashion items. They have a timelessness about them'.

Knitwear designer Catherine Bond wrote, 'Today, people are very fashion conscious and want things to be different and well-made'. Handcrafted accessories are valued because they are perceived as special and individualistic, unlike the mass produced object, estranged from its own production. Such objects often bear traces of the maker's 'thumbprint', a proof of the artisanal care taken. As Victoria Brown wrote, 'I have always been intrigued by the construction of 'proper' hats, the way they appear to have no beginning or end, the gold of the label printed into the lining of the crown and the funny little bow in the headband. Hats can seem very mysterious and perfect in their construction...until you start to pull them apart and find the glue and the huge stitches underneath'. Patrons of the bespoke accessory can also become further involved in its making by visiting workshop or designer and specifying their own design for, as John Lobb said, the most important thing about making shoes is 'to please the customer'. To wear handcrafted accessories reveals a desire not to be ordinary and identifies the individual with the ideals of the maker, for each object bears their aesthetic signature and excellence of craftsmanship which reaffirms the veracity of the wearer's choice.

The particular significance of handcrafted accessories is that every time they are worn, their qualities are reaffirmed through touch. In Natacha Marro's words, 'I find the magical thing about handmade shoes is making a one-off pair for a person that will fit them like a second skin and which they will be able to wear for many years as they become more and more a part of that person'. The sensation of touch, whether pleasurable or not, is a common memory of childhood amongst makers. The milliner Dai Rees recalled that 'my mother knitted a balaclava for me to wear; tight, coarse, tickly and grey', while Hikaru Noguchi wrote that she wanted her 'hats and bags to bring their owners happiness, like a cuddly toy does for a child'.

Putting on her 'Kiss of Death' hat Jo Gordon turned and bared her teeth, her face framed by a tunnel of black feathers, in a tableau which could have come from a Hitchcock film. It is this ability of accessories to inspire fondness, obsession, pleasure and even fear that inspires me and that I hope this exhibition gives voice to.

These ideas were realised by a Craft Council bursary, with the support of Valerie Mendes, Chief Curator of Textiles and Dress, Victoria and Albert Museum and Lou Taylor, Professor of Dress and Textile History, University of Brighton. Valerie Mendes wrote that 'Imaginatively conceived, meticulously crafted accessories are sources of enormous pleasure to both wearer and onlooker. To the historian they become ideal representatives of their period, revealing in their relatively small, portable and functional forms the skill and creativity of their makers, the taste of their owners and the social mores of their time. A handbag, hat or pair of shoes can operate on a number of visual levels, as the discreet finishing touch to an ensemble, the eye catching centre of attention or, in an entirely different dimension, stand alone as an independent piece of sculpture.' Professor Lou Taylor commented that, 'Perhaps we are now finally heading for the collapse of the great divides between the worlds of craft and fashion. It has taken all too long. The heart of the issue was that fashion was traditionally seen as ephemeral, commercial and even corrupting trivia both by fine artists, craft designers and even the protagonists of 'industrial art'. Since the mid-1980s, however, the bridge between fashion and crafts has been quietly building up. Now, pioneering designer-makers, teachers, retailers and alert consumers are successfully carrying this fusion of avant-garde fashion/craft skills and approaches from Britain to the heights of Paris couture.'

In displays of clothes and accessories nothing can substitute for the emotional presence of the living body. Just as we can never see the 'real' us at one glance, so the images we see of ourselves in this exhibition, formed by mirrors and shadows, are partial, the sounds and text impressionistic. In making reference to the part accessories play in our lives, this exhibition acknowledges their existence as objects in their own right, orbiting around us like the intense, solitary, highly crafted satellites of fashion that they are.

**Claire Wilcox**

A cold dining room in my grandmother's house. A table covered in decorative feathers, hats and hat-blocks. A child of six." **Jilli Blackwood**

"I love the idea of 'Glamour', making a woman feel special because she looks fantastic. The way that the practical need for a head covering is only a small part of what the hat is about. What it really signifies is fantasy, play acting, self expression, the idea that there is more to life than the mundane and practical aspects of our existence." **Pip Hackett**

"My first memory of a hat is of a white, fur helmet with ties and pom-poms. My sister and I wore these identical hats shopping with our mother."
**Anita Evagora of Fred Bare**

"I won a big hat competition when I was eight years old. I made a huge hat covered with blackberries and branches." Jo Gordon

"I have always been intrigued by the construction of 'proper' hats, the way they appear to have no beginning or end, the gold of the label printed into the lining of the crown and the funny little bow in the headband. Hats can seem very mysterious and perfect in their construction... until you start to pull them apart and find the glue and the huge stitches underneath."

Victoria Brown

"Crafts skills are paramount... particularly at the prototype stage. However I see no virtue in 'handmade' for it's own sake, if industrial technology is capable of the production." Sue Heathcote

# Soft Sculpture

The skills and interpretative processes of the objects in Satellites of Fashion depend
upon juxtaposing the traditional with the technological, the familiar with the obscene,
the synthetic with the organic to achieve an effect that is wholly other, ironic, alien
and very contemporary. It is a mood or ethos that causes us to look again – with
curiosity, discomfort, joy, anger or suspicion.

Of the exhibitors, Scott Wilson's head cages and beaded yashmaks have already
caused such reaction, for his pieces seem to emasculate the body or hide the face,
suggesting women in Purdah or souls in purgatory. Philip Treacy, on the other
hand, uses irony, juxtaposition and a sculptor's understanding of volume and form,
light and shade to produce effects that have won him the title 'The Rembrandt of
Millinery'. In contrast, Stephen Jones is never more effective than when using such
traditional materials as felt, fowl and spartre to produce hats that are truly Daliesque
and dazzling in their execution. Newcomer Flora McLean uses mesh, PVC, plastic,
felt, to produce a body of work that puzzles and gives pleasure equally. Sculptor
turned milliner Jo Gordon follows a more traditional route in the use of crafting
and materials – fleece, feathers, flocking – while the finished work impacts on the
senses like a Edith Sitwell poem or a Craigie Aitchison painting.

It is hardly surprising that galleries and museums around the world, from the
Kunst Museum in Germany, to the Kyoto Art Gallery in Japan, the Brooklyn Museum
in New York, and the Hayward, Barbican, and V&A in London have all exhibited
and purchased their work.

The placing of millinery within the milieu of sculpture or conceptual art is, however,
nothing new. Picasso coined the term 'soft sculpture' to describe the millinery and
dresses of Charles James, while Coco Chanel, who began life as a milliner, also looked
to the modern movement for inspiration, and numbered Picasso, Le Corbusier,
Marcel Breuer and Charlotte Perriand among her friends. She viewed her hats as
'pieces that embodied the spirits and freedoms of her time'. For Charles Worth, hats
were art, while Poiret merged art, design and commercialism when he founded the
Atelier Martine. This was a forerunner to Andy Warhol's factory, and contemporary
with Hoffman's Wiener Werkstatte, a place where hats, clothes, furniture and
tapestries amongst other things were crafted with an artist's attention to detail.
It was in this context that artist milliners such as Mme Paulette, Caroline Reboux,
Lilly Daché and Mr John, who was described as 'the artist among milliners' by

Eugina Sheppard of the New York Times, made their reputation for hats that were more metaphor than muslin, more art than artifice.

The impact of Surrealism on fashion and millinery is well documented. Marcel Duchamp used hat racks and racks that resembled hats to underscore the idea that objects need only be presented in a different way, or in a new context, to alter what they are, and how we should view them. Salvador Dali worked with Schiaparelli (who in turn used the talents of Christian Berard, Jean Cocteau and Louis Aragon) to produce hats and clothes that deliberately and successfully blurred the lines between millinery and sculpture, fashion and art. Like Jeff Koons, and Marcel Duchamp, Sarah Lucas and Tracy Emin, Schiaparelli plundered the products of the everyday – ice cream cones, lamb chops, shoes – to say something startling and new using that most intimate and personal of all gallery spaces, the head, to do it. This attitude is continued by some of the milliners in this exhibition, although Balenciaga, in the post-war period, was perhaps the first designer to define the head in such terms. He used forms and fabrics borrowed from architecture, Spanish painting and Japanese scroll work to create minimally massed pieces – in felt, leather, twigs, plastic, hessian and glass. These were described by Diane Vreeland as the 'perfect embodiments of form married to function,' terms normally saved for the artist and architect, rather that the designer and hatter.

The sixties, which gave voice to a new generation of artists and fashion designers was also the period that sounded the death knell for the milliner, especially those who tended towards the conceptual. This was the era of the 'youthquake', of ready-to-wear fashions, a time when women went hatless and models such as Twiggy and Penelope Tree frequented the saloon bar, rather than the salon. They were girls, when the models before them – such as Barbara Goalen or Bettina – were gloved goddesses who wore hats, and aloof expressions. Hats were deemed a bourgeois concept, the women who wore them and the designers that created them part of the ancien regime. During this time fashion became disposable, transient, a mirror that reflected on art, as in Yves St Laurent's Mondrian collection, rather than one that was part of it. Certainly there were hatters – Halston, Graham Smith, Frederick Fox, John Boyd, – but these were nursery slope candidates when compared to their couture predecessors, their pretensions of grandeur tempered by a climate ushered in by feminism and successive recessions which kept their feet and their hats firmly on the ground.

In the seventies' punk, Vivienne Westwood, Malcolm McLaren and the craft based dresses and head pieces of designers such as Zandra Rhodes and Andrew Logan inspired change. Trans-gender bands such as Japan and Spandau Ballet, artist-musicians such as David Bowie and Brian Eno saw performance as an artistic pursuit, once more elevated to the status of art. Hatters like Phillipe Model, Stephen Jones and David Shilling, designers such as Issey Miyake, Rei Kawakubo and Jean-Paul Gaultier discovered that *spectacle* was once more the way to go, for as Gaultier himself said, 'If art can be fashionable, why not vice versa'.

Doubtless, this has paved the way for today's batch of fast forward milliners – 3D artists and cultural surfers, who have no preconceptions and prejudices when it comes to exploring the true nature of the modern headpiece. Theirs is a world in which inspiration and references come from such diverse interests and disciplines as science, medicine, remixology, clubbing and sonic fiction. It is a world in which the works of J. G. Ballard and Irvine Welsh are more important than those of Cristobal Balenciaga and Coco Chanel; where the buildings of Zaha Hadid, or the dystopian cities of Branzi and Bladerunner have more in common with their outlooks and influences than even the most fantastic and inspiring pieces by Daché or Reboux.

It is no surprise that the work of such milliners has brought them in contact with designers such as Antonio Berardi, Alexander McQueen, Hussein Chalayan and Tristan Webber, all of whom have forsaken the blandness of the catwalk for 'happenings', 'installations', 'performances' and A/V spectacles that have more in common with the world of art than that of the world of fashion. It is in this context that much of Satellites of Fashion should be viewed: hats for heads certainly, but hats for heads that have been educated in the culture via magazines like Dazed, Dutch and IT rather than Vogue or Harpers Bazaar.

**Martin Raymond**

"A red plastic toy medical kit bag – the plasticky smell, the shiny almost sticky red exterior, the pockets and fittings inside for the plastic apparatus and the shiny gold clicky clasp."
Sarah Crawford

"I used to go up to London for the day with my mother and she would wear a patent handbag and white gloves and matching shoes so when the patent handbag came out it meant excitement and going to London. I always remember my mother's handbag full of blotted lipstick tissues and that lovely powdery smell." Lulu Guiness

"Craft for me is not the end product, but just a word to describe 'the making process'. The craft of designing and experimentation, pattern making, creating a maquette, alterations, and production of the final article...this is the craft of fashion." Louise Barber

"We have no machinery, because you can't improve on hand-stitching. "
Neil MacGregor and Valerie Michael

"My earliest memory of a bag is of my Slovenian grandmother handing me a mushroom picking bag made out of straw." Sonia Boriczewski

# Private Worlds in Public Places

'The train slows and lengthens, as we approach London, the centre, and my heart draws out too, in fear, in exultation...The huge uproar is in my ears. It sounds and resounds under this glass roof like the surge of the sea. We are cast down on the platform with our handbags. We are whirled asunder. My sense of self almost perishes; my contempt. I become drawn in, tossed down, thrown sky-high. I step out onto the platform, grasping tightly all that I possess – one bag.' Virginia Woolf, 'The Waves', 1931

The history of the bag is inextricably linked with travel, but its development also expresses the metaphorical journeys that women have undertaken this century. Diminutive versions of travelling bags dominated women's handbag styles in the late nineteenth century, alluding to the security and strength of luggage and many had ornate metal clasps with tiny locks and keys. Bags became increasingly sophisticated, with internal fittings for cosmetics and matching 'chained' purses, while for the priviledged there were exquisitely made cases with fan, powder puff, smelling salts and opera glasses. By the 1930s, handbags were seen as objects of flirtation; fashion was focused on the sensuous, sophisticated woman rather than the boyish 'flapper' with her fringed, beaded bag. The pochette (for the bag had temporarily lost its handle) provided a focal point, a reminder of the womanliness of the owner. It soon became second nature to use handbags to draw attention to a slender wrist, or, placed discretely on the floor, to a well-turned ankle. After the Second World War the freedom that women had gained, epitomised by the practical shoulder bag, was replaced by a preoccupation with femininity and domesticity. Etiquette books and fashion manuals prevailed, driven by an inner concern with outward appearances. 'A good handbag is something one can afford to be snobbish about; it is so very much a sign of good grooming. A real tell-tale, open or shut'. ('Accent on Accessories', 1957)

In the 1960s, daughters rejected the idea of dressing like their mothers and the formal handbag became a symbol of the past. The poet Adrienne Rich wrote that 'Mother stands for the victim in ourselves, the unfree woman...We develop matrophobia and try to split ourselves off from her...in a desperate attempt to know where mother ends and daughter begins'. Bags were no longer considered as investments and cheap plastics meant that styles could change rapidly, as youth fashions and 'ready-to-wear' began to dominate. By the 1970s, a new romanticism had emerged. Ethnic styles and long skirts were complimented by tiny Indian purses, worn diagonally across the body. In 1973 I wore one to a Grateful Dead concert, it contained a bottle of patchouli oil and my train fare home, but the string broke. I could not find it in the dark, crowded

25

concert hall, and felt suddenly, profoundly lost. Large, secure shoulder bags became survival kits for urban living, containing everything from lunch to a change of clothes for after work. It was not until the affluent 1980s that the social and work related functions of the bag separated into designer label handbags or briefcases, which took their inspiration from menswear.

Today, the variety of receptacles, from rucksack to tiny evening bag, expresses the wide choice of journeys to be made. The range of bags in this exhibition show how craft makers have responded to those needs. Sonia Boriczewski wrote that 'The most important thing to me about making bags is to create something that people can not only use, but which is also visually and texturally interesting. Something that makes people stop and look again, at an everyday object transformed'. Each maker in Satellites of Fashion plots their own path; while Sharon Porteous alludes to transience and regeneration in her recycled carriers, Asta Barrington's embroidered bags and Hikaru Noguchi and Sonia Boriczewski' s knitted bags recall the fabric receptacles of the last century, lovingly crafted at home, the passing of time documented with every stitch. The fluidity of Bill Amberg's work complements that of Neil MacGregor and Valerie Michael, direct descendants of the British saddlery tradition; both equip and protect us for many journeys, and with each, bag and wearer become more intimate. Some bags suggest a journey of dreams, others a secret rendezvous. Such assignations are suggested by Emily Jo Gibb's tiny silk and metal purses, which would hold no more than a scrap of a handkerchief or Lulu Guinness' bags, perhaps a scented envelope tucked inside. Louise Barber's mesh purses convey a sense of mystery, even unease, they could enclose a single postage stamp or a secret message. Still others create a sense of dignity as in Nathalie Hambro's mesh boxes, or Ignacio and Corral's woven silk forms, while Sarah Crawford's large plastic structures, bright and bristling, shock us to laughter.

Bags are personal, and the memories they contain are particular to each generation. While the poet Ruth Fainlight's mother carried letters from her father, "softened and worn at the edges, opened, read, and refolded so often" others inspire fear, possess sinister qualities, connected perhaps with their secrecy; a friend recalled as a small child being terrified of his mother's handbag. "It was a container that I wasn't allowed to go inside, and somehow it contained the essence of femininity and adult-hood, it was charged with mystery". Emily Jo Gibbs remembered 'a large red vinyl shopping bag...I can remember very clearly her coming down the street with it', while

Sonia Boriczewski's first memory was of 'my Slovenian grandmother handing me a mushroom picking bag made out of straw'. These journeys back in time are evoked by memories of bags; it seems obvious to say that childhood lays down the tactile and visual experience which informs the rest of our conscious lives.

Fashion is a powerful force, and it is often used to reinvent ourselves. Emptying out an old and filling a new bag is intensely pleasurable, for the handbag colludes with our sense of a fresh start. Handbags become friends, they will not betray their wearer by causing blisters, or falling off. Ever since handbags have become part of fashion they have helped to define our individuality and identity, for as Simone de Beauvoir wrote in 'The Second Sex' (1949) 'To care for her beauty, to dress up, is a kind of work that enables her to take possession of her person'.

In Katherine Mansfield's short story 'The Escape', published in 1920, a couple find their relationship pushed to its limits while travelling abroad. He sees her as if for the first time, through her open handbag: 'The little bag, with its shiny, silvery jaws open, lay on her lap. He could see her powder-puff, her rouge stick, a bundle of letters, a phial of tiny black pills like seeds, a broken cigarette, a mirror, white ivory tablets with lists on them that had been heavily scored through. He thought: 'In Egypt she would have been buried with these things.'

While every material object we choose reinforces a sense of self, the handbag has a particular significance, for it is connected to a private self-awareness, showing one thing, but hiding another. Because of the dual lives that we lead, between public and private, past and present, we struggle to express what we know we are and what we are supposed to be. Bags exemplify this dichotomy, the tension between internal and external existence. They do not clothe the body, yet they provide a portable refuge, bearing the things we value and need, love letter or map, keys to home or plane ticket, transporting our private worlds into public places.

**Claire Wilcox**

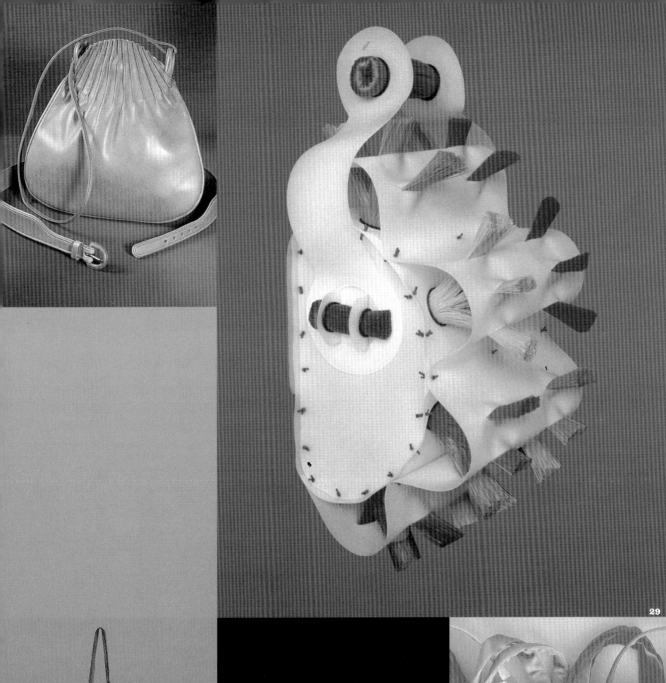

"My earliest memory is a dream where someone had given me a huge chest full of shoes and when I woke up I was bitterly disappointed."
**Henrietta Park**

"'Fashion' is part of the dream we sell; the dream doesn't work without quality and fit...'The Craft.'"
**Oliver Sweeney**

"My typical customer is someone looking for an alternative look, someone with an established style and mature attitude to fashion, who enjoys the fit and comfort of made to measure."
**Natacha Marro**

"I used to shut myself in my mother's wardrobe and try on all her shoes." Paul Thomas

"Measuring feet, taking a draft, design, clicking, pattern cutting, last fitting, handskiving." Joanna Walker

"I visualise the characters in the novels I read… and then imagine their shoes. Their shoes are my shoes." Ghita Schuy

"Shoes are very 3-dimensional objects when not worn – they don't need the body to give them form. Feelings experienced and communicated by the wearer seem to be possessed by shoes." Nicola Lawler

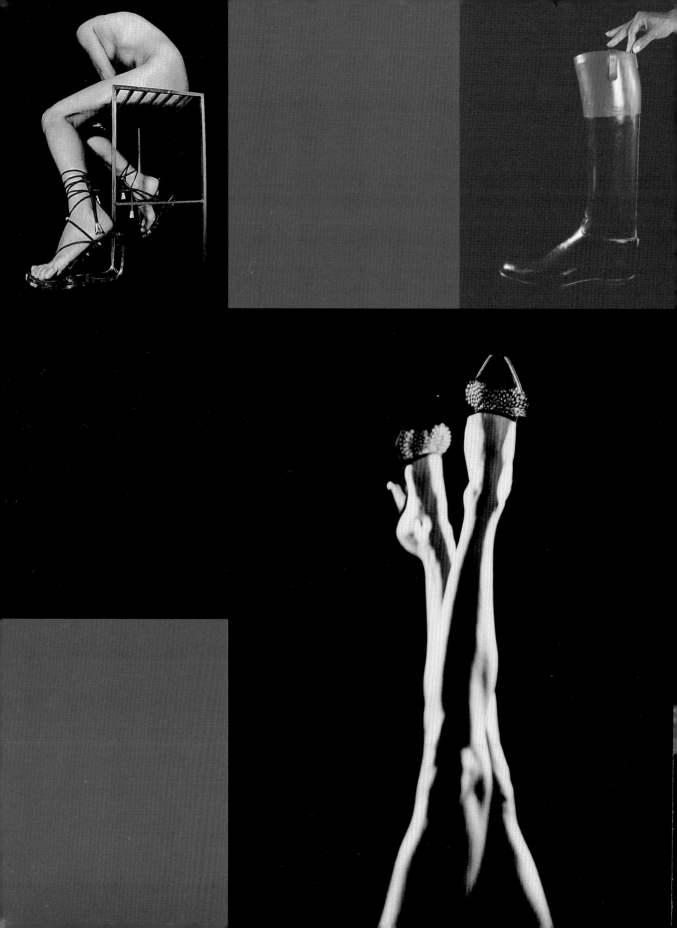

# New Shoes

"At one time, according to Sir George Darwin the moon was very close to the earth. Then the tides gradually pushed her far away: the tides that the moon herself causes in the earth's waters...Orbit? Oh elliptical of course: for a while it would huddle against us and then it would take flight for a while. The tides when the moon swung closer, rose so high nobody could hold them back" Italo Calvino, 'Cosmicomics'.

The moon, earth's satellite, pursues its eccentric orbit and rotates at the same rate about its own axis. The changing, reflected crescents of our satellite are only one side, the other 'dark side' of the moon, until recently a mystery to mankind. On earth the swell of tides is attenuated by the lunar influence and in its turn the moon slowly gains its independence. Fashion's satellites, in this instance shoes, participate in the same rhythms, the same seasonal changes as a larger fashion system (meaning both a complete style or 'look' and a wider economic reality) in whose gravitational pull they are situated. The designers of shoes, masters of an increasingly independent craft, have often been overshadowed by those whose collections they accessorise. In this exhibition they are given names.

Shoes have presented a problem within traditional exhibitions of dress. Their presence is essential to the completion of a look but they are often replaced by reproductions, drilled through their base and bolted to the mannequin's supporting pedestal or represented by forms cast to the feet of the mannequin itself with any decoration or style painted on. The exhibition of original examples has relied on their inherent sculptural qualities. Relegated to a side (and often crowded) glass cabinet, at eye level, the object/shoe distinction is blurred. Here, they reverently float just above the ground maintaining their primacy as shoes; our identification is immediate.

This exhibition exists here and now. The specificity of the brief removed the need for a contextual, thematic, or historical prelude or chosen chronological route. Each pair of shoes exists in the same time, the same place. The viewer is already dressed for these shoes, increasing the fantasy of ownership; they are both wearable and collectable, both exquisite under the spot light and at home on the London pavement outside the gallery, both *already* and *still* in 'fashion'. Nostalgia belongs to the dreams of the viewer; the display places us on the threshold of a daydream.

A large number of the exhibitors were drawn to London to complete their Diploma at Cordwainers College or to gain their expertise as apprentices at the bespoke

35

meccas, remaining to participate in an ever growing avant-garde scene, with the clientele it brings and the possibilities for collaboration. Many work counter to the economics of mass production which relies on standardised lasts; the participants in the exhibition represent highly skilled, individualistic designers at the forefront of international trends. Reflecting a greater continuum in the design of men's shoes than their more socially and morally complex feminine counterparts, perhaps the shoes that most accurately represent the culmination of generations of bespoke bootmakers are those by John Lobb. As with couture, the layering of specialist intervention (from fitter, last maker, clicker, closer, maker and polisher) betrays the painstaking accuracy of this craft. Totally individual, their client lists read like a Who's Who of the 20th century, from Frank Sinatra to the famous lover of shoes, the Duke of Windsor. If Lobb signifies tradition, then both Oliver Sweeney and Patrick Cox have provided the classic loafer with a twist, instantly recognisable to all 'wannabes'.

It is however women's accessories that dominate the exhibition, taking the skills of traditional shoemaking and applying to them a vocal and contemporary language. The prop essential to every little girl's dressing up box takes us on numerous fantastic journeys, we can play at being nymphs or valkyries. Beads, buckles, leatherwork, metalwork and delicate embroidery create motifs invested in ideas beyond our field of vision with overwhelming plurality, each speak a sophisticated language of subversion. History finds its way into a dictionary of taste, we find Ferragamo's S-shaped heel from 1947 applied to a patent boot, ruby slippers worthy of Manet's Olympia, or the flag from Camille di Mauro's Liberation Shoe of 1944 on a unisex loafer. Among the exhibits in Satellites of Fashion holographic plastic plays a witty game as it camouflages our toes with butterflies as they lift from the ground, and bedded with roses when in repose, belonging both to heaven and to earth. We are lifted intentionally forward and rewarded with height, as a sheriff's badge, a symbol of strict authority, becomes a five spiked heel.

Always a couple, both an interdependent unit and a complicit duality, one shoe acts as a mirror to its partner; equal, the idea of original and copy is subverted. These tiny canvases become imperative to a season's fashion and betray the minute precision with which shoes are created. The tides of style are reflected by the decorative uppers, the height and width of the heel and the acuteness of the angle of the toe. Only a few millimetres determine security from discomfort, fashion from masquerade.

Both intimate and very public, shoes inhabit the geography of limits. Shoes present both a point of contact with the world and our immediate shield from it. 'Outside and inside for a dialectic of division, the obvious geometry of which blinds us as soon as we bring it into play in metaphorical domains. It has the sharpness of the dialectic of *yes* and *no*, which decides everything' (Gaston Bachelard 'The Poetics of Space Ch.9 p.211 Beacon Press, Boston, 1969) The shod foot is always more erotic than the naked foot, free to breathe unadorned. Shoes signify the secrecy of enclosure – the peep toe holds the excitement of a peep-show, relying on the transfer of the metaphysics of dressed to undressed, soft flesh and hard surface, the inert and the living. Whereas 'holes' piercing the uppers of shoes are titillating to many, those through the sole present a crisis, like a leak in the sacred, intimate space of our home, it corrupts an absolute code – we are no longer shielded from the chaos of the city.

'What is more beautiful than a road? It is the symbol of an active and varied life' (Georges Sand, 'Consuelo', vol II p.116). Dirt personalises shoes. The shoes on display are not only current, but new. All dirt associated with wear, both inside and underneath is absent. The shoes are waiting for the heat from our feet to mould the inside, their movement to scratch the memories of travel on the sole, and at the same moment leave a trace, or a footprint behind. Despite a rise in the purchase of vintage couture, auction houses confirm a problem with selling shoes. Those from the recent past are difficult to sell, and are valued more as memorabilia than as vintage dress. Who has been in them, and where have they been? Dirt is present inside and out, however beautiful the design.

It is the exhibition and documentation of shoes which places them in the orbit of collectables. In 1996, at the first ever Biennale of fashion, Manolo Blahnik alone carried the shoemakers' art into the Palazzo Vecchio in Florence. It was Blahnik who acknowledged in his preface to Colin McDowell's seminal book 'Shoes, Fashion and Fantasy' a decade ago, the birth of a new generation of shoe makers, amongst whom we may find the new Yantourmi, Perugia or Rivier. Here we celebrate that group. For the 1998 Biennale the theme of Cinderella dominates the 13 rooms of the Palazzo Spini Feroni hosted by the Salvatore Ferragamo Museum, as we celebrate the centenary of the birth of Ferragamo, one of the great shoe designers of the 20th century, together with the centenary of the first film of Cinderella. It is now fashion's turn to pay homage to this tale.

**Judith Clark**

# Exhibits List

All dimensions are in cms
(height, width, depth)

**1**
**Fred Bare**
Norwegian Hat
January 1998
100% wool knit, 100% viscose fur
29 x 30 x 30

**2**
**Fred Bare**
Helmet
January 1998
100% wool crochet, 100%
viscose fur
30 x 28 x 26

**3**
**Jilli Blackwood**
Embroidered Hat
1998
Hand-dyed silks, velvets,
muslins, embroidery, woven
and clipped fabric

**4**
**Jilli Blackwood**
Embroidered Hat
1998
Hand-dyed silks, velvets,
muslins, embroidery, woven
and clipped fabric

**5**
**Jilli Blackwood**
Embroidered Hat
1998
Hand-dyed silks, velvets,
muslins, embroidery, woven
and clipped fabric

**6**
**Catherine Bond**
Rasta Hat
August 1998
Pure new wool, viscose
Knitted, corded and twisted
rastas
45 Height

**7**
**Catherine Bond**
Sculptured Hat
August 1998
Pure new wool, bouclé mix
Knitted with 27 Rectangles
40 Height

**8**
**Catherine Bond**
Patchwork Hat
August 1998
Pure new wool Knitted with
printed pieces of knit
33 Height

**9**
**Victoria Brown**
Multi Patterned Hat
August 1998
Hand rolled wool felt and
gold leaf
32 x 30 x 33

**10**
**Victoria Brown**
Pink with Blue Spot Hat
August 1998
Hand rolled wool felt and
gold leaf
33 x 30 x 33

**11**
**Victoria Brown**
Blues with Silver Hat
August 1998
Hand rolled wool felt and
silver leaf
33 x 33 x 33

**12**
**Victoria Brown**
Pink with Stripes Hat
August 1998
Hand rolled wool felt and
gold leaf
30 x 30 x 33

**13**
**Jo Gordon**
Beaded hat
July 1998
10,000 haematite beads,
dentistry wire
50 x 50 x 30
Commission piece for Crafts
Council

**14**
**Jo Gordon**
Dandelion hat
July 1998
Ostrich feathers, spartre and
flocking
50 x 40 x 50

**15**
**Pip Hackett**
Twin Peaks
June 1998
Millinery canvas, wire, tarlatan,
felt holographic sequins
25 x 8
Designs for Life. Inspired by
the red ribbon symbol.
Specially commissioned by
London Lighthouse for
Fashion Show, Summer 1998

**16**
**Pip Hackett**
Midsummer Nights Dream
May 1997
Spartre, wire, satin backed
crepe, antique bird of paradise
and curved pheasant feathers
20.3 x 45.7

**17**
**Sue Heathcote**
Hat 1
1998
2/15's lambswool
Knitted, intarsia, felted finish
18 x 52

18
Sue Heathcote
Hat 2
1998
2/15's lambswool
Knitted, intarsia, felted finish
18 x 52

19
Stephen Jones
Cork Street
Autumn/Winter 1998
Styrofoam and flock
20 x 15 x 2

20
Stephen Jones
Aether
Spring/Summer 1998
Metal and silk
35 x 15 x 15

21
Stephen Jones
Creation
Spring/Summer 1998
Satin, suede, perspex and
diamanté
20 x 10 x 2

22
Flora McLean
Wind and Rain Visor
February 1998
Polythene
Laminating and heat sealing,
welding
35 x 30

23
Flora McLean
Red PVC Norwester
February 1998
Red PVC
Sewn
11 x 60 x 33

24
Flora McLean
Turquoise Towelling Beret
June 1998
Towelling, pipe cleaners
Sewing, modelling
12 x 16 x 16

25
Dai Rees
Pheasant Quill Hat
August 1998
Human hair, blossom head piece
60 x 40 x 40
Commission piece for Crafts
Council

26
Dai Rees
Ant Eater, Tailed Hat
August/September 1998
Feather quills, reconstructed
peacock feathers, synamay
60 x 40 x 40

27
Dai Rees
Quills in Flight
August/September 1998
Feather quills
60 x 40 x 40

28
Rachel Skinner
Purple Heart
March 1998
Silk velvet, pheasant feathers
and veiling
12.7 x 30.5 x 30.5

29
Rachel Skinner
Feathered Hat
1998

30
Adele Tipler
Hat
1998
Electroformed copper wire
25 x 25 x 25
Commission piece for Crafts
Council

31
Adele Tipler
Hat
1998
Electroformed copper wire,
silver plate
Soldered and electroformed
20 x  20 x 25

32
Philip Treacy
Feather Union Jack Hat
November 1996

33
Philip Treacy
Show Hat
Autumn/Winter 1997
Red wool-mix disc hat, single
black quill, black satin ribbon

34
Scott Wilson
Sphere
September 1998
Mirrorised perspex
Cutting, filling, polishing,
mirrorising surface
45 x 35

35
Scott Wilson
Mask
September 1998
Perspex, formed and shaped,
cut, filed, polished
20 x 26 x 9

36
Ignacio and Corral
Satin Square Metallic Handbag
1998
Woven lurex
23 x 23

37
Ignacio and Corral
Green Envelope Bag
1998
Handbag laid and stitched Jute
34 x 35

38
Ignacio and Corral
Black Sphere Handbag
1998
3-D deformed woven linen
13 x 50

39
Bill Amberg
Fish Basket
September 1998
Bridle leather, yew wood handle
Wood carving and polishing,
weaving, edge polishing
Commission piece for Crafts
Council

40
Bill Amberg
St Tropez Portrait Bag
August 1998
Bridle leather, suede lining
Hand-cutting and hand
polished edges
29 x 33 x 6

41
Louise Barber
Bronze Pleated Roll-Up Bag
1998
Patinated phosphor bronze
mesh. Brass rectangular sec-
tion wire oxidised and waxed
21.5 x 9 x 6.5

42
Louise Barber
Metal Mesh Bag
1998
Oxidised phosphor bronze mesh,
silver rivet detail and clip
15 x 29 x 3

43
Louise Barber
Silver and Steel No. 1
1998
Stainless steel mesh, hand
pleated, silver rivet details and
handles
30 x 36 x 1
Commission piece for Crafts
Council

44
Asta Barrington
Baroque Bag
1998
Viscose, rayon, satin
18 x 19.5 x 2.5

45
Asta Barrington
Circles Bag
1998
Viscose, rayon, satin
17 x 20 x 2

46
Asta Barrington
Spiral Bag
1998
Viscose, rayon, satin
18 x 18 x 2.5

47
Sonia Boriczewski
Paper Bag 1
July 1998
Paper yarn
Machine knitted, hand finished
87 x 29 x 5

48
Sonia Boriczewski
Paper Bag 2
July 1998
Paper yarn
Machine knitted, hand finished
87 x 29 x 5

49
Sarah Crawford
Scrubbing Brush Bag VI
August 1998
Nylon sheet and scrubbing
brushes, rubber rings, elastic
fishing line
40 x 25 x 45

50
Sarah Crawford
Scrubbing Brush Bag VII
August 1998
Nylon sheet, nylon scrubbing
brushes,
rubber rings, elastic fishing line
40 x 25 x 45

51
Emily Jo Gibbs
Perspex Handled Bag
1997
Wool, silk, perspex, cotton
interlining
23.5 x 15 x 8

52
Emily Jo Gibbs
Sun Bag
1997
Sterling silver, silk, metallic
cloth
Cast pieces soldered on to wire,
hand sewn to bag
16 x 2

**53**
**Emily Jo Gibbs**
Copper Disc Bag
1998
Copper, silk, gold plate,
viscose cord
Handcut and beaten disks
sewn to bag, gold plated silver
soldered frame
16 x 12 x 3

**54**
**Emily Jo Gibbs**
Dandelion Bag
1997
Sterling silver, blocking net,
organza. Cast pieces sewn on to
blocked domes, silver soldered
hinge, frame, and clasp sewn
to domes
10 Diameter

**55**
**Emily Jo Gibbs**
Pebble Bag
1998
Mixed metals, silk organza,
blocking net
Metal decoration and frame
sewn on to silk covered blacked
shapes
Commission piece for Crafts
Council

**56**
**Lulu Guinness**
Spider Web
August 1998
Satin, embroidery, nickel
31 x 18 x 4

**57**
**Lulu Guinness**
Fan
September 1998
Satin and silk thread
embroidery
13.5 x 18 x 4

**58**
**Nathalie Hambro**
Bucket Bag II
May 1998
Brass gauze, shantung,
iridescent glass beads, copper
dust, enamelled wire
28 x 19 x 15

**59**
**Nathalie Hambro**
Inro Bag
May 1998
Stainless steel gauze, embossed
lead sheets

**60**
**Neil MacGregor**
(MacGregor and Michael)
Three Corners Bag
September 1998
Latigo cow hide and linen
thread
41 x 16 x 8

**61**
**Valerie Michael**
(MacGregor and Michael)
Shoulder Bag
September 1998
Latigo cow hide
26 x 20 x 6

**62**
**Valerie Michael**
(MacGregor and Michael)
Waist bag
September 1998
Latigo cow hide
20 x 16

**63**
**Hikaru Noguchi**
Bubbly Bag
October 1996
100% wool
Knitted
32 x 25 x 6

**64**
**Hikaru Noguchi**
Red Indian Bag
February 1998
50% angora, 50% lambswool
Knitted
35 x 20 x 10

**65**
**Sharon Porteous**
Classic Carrier
(semi transparent)
August 1998
Waste plastic carrier bags,
reclaimed yarn
Hand woven, heat pressed
43 x 28 x 13
Commission piece for Crafts
Council

**66**
**Sharon Porteous**
Classic Carrier (white)
August 1998
Waste plastic carrier bags,
reclaimed yarn
Hand woven, heat pressed
43 x 28 x 13

**67**
**Sharon Porteous**
Classic Carrier
(semi transparent)
August 1998
Waste plastic carrier bags,
reclaimed yarn
Hand woven, heat pressed
23 x 20 x 10

**68**
**Manolo Blahnik**
Soya
Spring 1997
Satin, ostrich plumes
**69**
**Manolo Blahnik**
Ladies Shoes
Black suede, feathers

**70**
**Rachel Bratt**
Ladies's Shoes
1998
Woven constucted fabrics:
fibre content, cotton and nylon
monofiliment, leather sole
**71**
**Rachel Bratt**
Ladies's Shoes
1998
Woven constucted fabrics:
fibre content, cotton and nylon
monofiliment, leather sole

**72**
**Jimmy Choo**
Pearl Beaded Shoes
August 1998
Satin uppers with silk ribbon,
Pearl detail and leather lining
**73**
**Jimmy Choo**
Pewter Beaded Mules
August 1998
Silk taffeta uppers, pewter
beading, leather lining

**74**
**Patrick Cox**
Loafer
1998
Anaconda skin

**75**
**Patrick Cox**
Perspex Wedge
1998
Perspex, crepe

**76**
**Emma Hope**
3D Kitten Heel Mules
Spring/Summer 1998 Collection
Plastic, leather upper, leather
sole
**77**
**Emma Hope**
Oyster Satin Embroidered
Boots
Autumn/Winter 1998/99
Collection
Silk upper, leather sole

**78**
**Nicola Lawler** (for Ghost)
Bad Fairy
September 1998
Black leather
**79**
**Nicola Lawler** (for Ghost)
Fairy Boot
September 1998
Cream leather upper and lin-
ing, black sole

**80**
**John Lobb, Bootmaker**
Hunting Boot
1968
Calf and hide leather
(Beechwood Tree)
**81**
**John Lobb, Bootmaker**
Russian Calf Half Brogue Oxford
1955
Calfskin upper, oak bark tanned
hide sole, mahogany tree

**82**
**John Lobb, Bootmaker**
Patent Dress Pump
1988
Black patent calf upper,
oak bark tanned hide sole,
mahogany tree

**83**
**Natacha Marro**
Mae West Cowboy Boots
February 1995
Leather upper and sole, silver
plated heel, silver fork
Thanks to Andrew Hapeshis
**84**
**Natacha Marro**
Donkey Boots
Winter 97/98
Goat skin, leather
Thanks to Andrew Hapeshis

**85**
**Henrietta Park**
Two Tone Sling Backs
June 1998
Blue and cream calf
**86**
**Henrietta Park**
Knee High Boots
July 1998
Green calf
Commission piece for Crafts
Council

**87**
**Ghita Schuy**
Widmer (Ladies Shoes)
September 1998
Black leather, blue fabric
**88**
**Ghita Schuy**
Zadek (Mens Shoes)
September 1998

89
Oliver Sweeney
Soho (lace boot)
1/2/98
Leather, swing welt soles
Blake shoe construction
90
Oliver Sweeney
Kensington (loafer)
1/2/98
Leather, swing welt soles
Blake shoe construction

91
Paul Thomas
Boot 2000
September 1998
Holographic leather upper,
clear perspex heel, silver plated
razor wire
Commission piece for Crafts
Council
92
Paul Thomas
Jester Shoe
July 1998
Leather and beech wood

93
Joanna Walker
Fitted Ladies Two Tone Boots
1998
Black leather kid, green side calf
Leather lining, handmade heel-
covered in black leather kid
Commission piece for Crafts
Council
94
Joanna Walker
Open Toe Boot
Black kid, leather kid lining,
handmade wooden heels
leather insoles and soles

95
Vivienne Westwood
Platform Shoes


Details correct at time of going
to press

# Credits

**Exhibition**

Curator
Claire Wilcox

Exhibition organiser
Beatrice Hosegood

Exhibition design
Urban Salon

Exhibition soundtrack
composer
Richard Walmsley

Exhibition graphics
Cartlidge Levene

**Catalogue**

Catalogue design
Pentagram

Cover photograph
Sara Morris

Chapter divider photographs
Gry Garness
Hats (pages 10 and 11):
Pip Hackett 'Twin Peaks' 1998
Bags (pages 20 and 21):
Emily Jo Gibbs
'Dandelion Bag' 1997
Shoes (pages 30 and 31):
Jimmy Choo
'Pearl Beaded Shoes' 1998

Printers
Colortec

ISBN
1 870 145 79 8

# Tour dates

## Exhibition dates

Crafts Council Gallery
22 October 1998 to
10 January 1999

Crafts Council
44a Pentonville Road
London N1 9BY

## Tour dates

13 February to 1 May 1999
Firstsite at the Minories
74 High Street
Colchester CO1 1UE
Tel 01206 577067
Contact: Katherine Wood,
Executive Director

25 September to
21 November 1999
Castle Museum
Nottingham NG1 6EL
Tel 0115 9153656
Contact: Christine Wall,
Acting Exhibition Officer

27 November 1999 to 23
January 2000
Northhampton Museum
and Art Gallery
Guildhall Road
Northampton NN1 1DP
Tel 01604 233500
Contact: Sheila Stone, Curator
and Mark Curteis,
Head of Interpretation